P9-DUE-415

MY FIRST SKETCHBOOK

DRAWING MONSTERS

A Step-by-Step Sketchbook

by Mari Bolte
illustrated by Lucy Makuc

CAPSTONE PRESS
a capstone imprint

First Facts are published by Capstone Press,
1710 Roe Crest Drive, North Mankato, Minnesota 56003
www.capstonepub.com

Library of Congress Cataloging-in-Publication Data
Bolte, Mari., author.
 Drawing monsters : a step-by-step sketchbook / by Mari Bolte ; illustrated by Lucy Makuc.
    pages cm. — (First facts. My first sketchbook)
 Summary: "Step-by-step instructions and sketches show how to draw a variety of spooky
and silly monsters"—Provided by publisher.
 ISBN 978-1-4914-0282-5 (library binding)
 ISBN 978-1-4914-0287-0 (eBook PDF)
1. Monsters in art—Juvenile literature. 2. Drawing—Technique—Juvenile literature. I.
Makuc, Lucy, illustrator. II. Title.
 NC825.M6B65 2015
 743.87—dc23   2014013815

Editorial Credits
Juliette Peters, designer; Katy LaVigne, production specialist

Photo Credits
Capstone Studio: Karon Dubke, 5 (photos); Shutterstock: Azuzl (design element),
Kalenik Hannah (design element), oculo (design element)

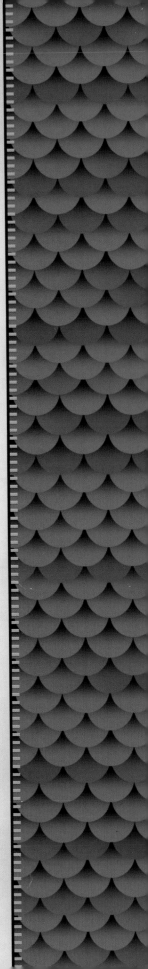

Printed in the United States of America in North Mankato, Minnesota.
042014   008087CGF14

Table of Contents

Make Me a Monster....................... 4

Furry Friend 6

I See You!... 8

Bug Eye 10

Lots of Legs 12

Nice Nessie...................................... 14

Monster Under the Bed............. 16

Say "Yes" to Yetis! 18

Fangy Friend 20

Deep Sea Diver 22

Read More..................................24

Internet Sites.............................24

Make Me a Monster

Some monsters are scary
and want to spook you.
But others are cuddly
and super cute too!

Don't scream if you don't know where to begin.
This book is just for you. Follow these tips and the
simple steps on each page. You'll be drawing the cutest
monsters ever in no time.

TIP 1 **Draw lightly.** You will need to erase some
lines as you go, so draw them light.

TIP 2 **Add details.** Little details, such as scales or
horns, make your monsters come to life.

TIP 3 **Color your drawings.** Color can make a flat
monster pop off the page!

You won't need tentacles or extra eyes.
But you will need some supplies.

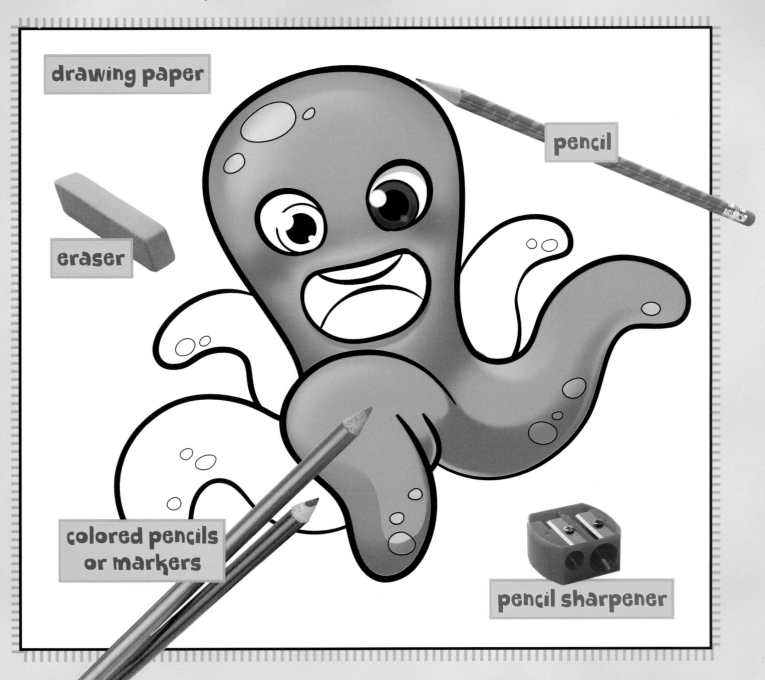

drawing paper

pencil

eraser

colored pencils
or markers

pencil sharpener

Sharpen your pencils, and get ready to draw
all monsters strange, silly, and scary. **It will be a
monstrously fun time!**

Furry Friend

Furry monsters are the friendliest! Give this shaggy fuzzball a fluffy mop of hair.

Final

Draw a large circle. Draw two smaller circles and a narrow half-circle inside.

Don't Forget!
Erase lines that go under something else. For example, erase the round circle you drew in step 1 after you add hair.

Draw scalloped lines around the large circle for hair. Add two small circles for eyes.

Add detail lines to give your monster personality. Add two small circles inside the eyes for pupils.

I See You!

This little monster is doing a happy dance. Maybe he's happy because he's so cute!

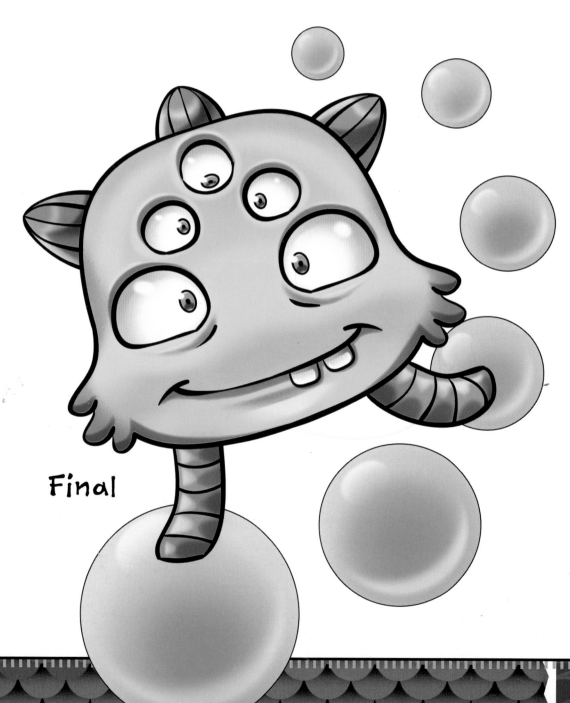

Final

1

Draw a square shape. Add two circles for eyes. Add two rounded lines for legs. Draw three lines where the monster's horns will be.

2

Add two circles above the first pair of eyes. Add little circles inside the larger eyes. Draw scalloped lines on the sides of the body for fur. Then draw a smile line.

3

Draw curved lines over the three horn lines from Step 1. Add another circle for the monster's fifth eye.

4

Add little circles inside the rest of the eyes. Sketch detail lines on the monster's horns, feet, and face. Add two curved lines for teeth.

Bug Eye

This little bug is ready to scurry across the page. Can your pencil keep up?

Final

1

Draw a curved bean shape. Add a circle for an eye and a square shape for a mouth. Sketch a detail line across the top third of the square for top teeth.

2

Draw three thin ovals for tentacles. Add some half-circles at the bottom of the bug's body to start the feet. A few sketch lines add detail to the bug's mouth and eye.

3

Draw three more tentacles on the other side of the monster's face. Finish the bug's feet by making the half-circles from Step 2 into long ovals. Draw a circle for the eye's pupil and a couple more detail lines.

Lots of Legs

This sweet surfing sea creature is having a great time. You'll have a great time drawing him too!

Final

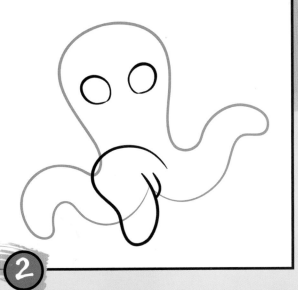

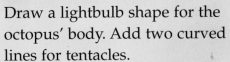

1

Draw a lightbulb shape for the octopus' body. Add two curved lines for tentacles.

2

Add two circles for eyes. Draw a curved line for another tentacle.

3

Add two more curved lines for the remaining tentacles. Draw two circles inside the eyes for pupils. Give your monster a mouth too.

4

Draw small bubbly circles all over the monster. Add detail lines inside the monster's mouth and small circles inside the eyes.

Nice Nessie

The Loch Ness Monster is real—and adorable! Draw this legendary cutie who just wants to be found.

Final

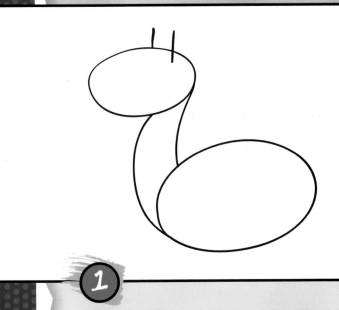

1

Draw a large oval for a body and a smaller oval for a head. Connect the ovals with two curved lines. Sketch two lines on the top of the head.

2

Sketch some curved lines to give Nessie's face a shape. Add detail lines to the antenna lines from Step 1. Add curved lines for Nessie's tail, and a circle for an eye.

3

Draw a circle for the monster's pupil. Add detail lines on Nessie's face, and draw curved lines for front flippers.

4

Add detail lines along Nessie's belly, and add a smile. Draw a little teardrop shape for Nessie's nose.

Monster Under the Bed

This monster under the bed isn't scary at all. Draw a friendly face to peek at in the middle of the night.

Final

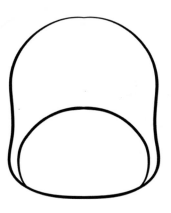

1 Draw an oval for the body. Draw a smaller oval inside and at the bottom of the first oval.

2 Add some scalloped detail lines for the monster's fur. Draw two curved lines for arms. Use a curved line to add a mouth.

3 Add more scalloped detail lines for hair. Then add two pointed ovals for horns and two half-circles for feet. Draw a tiny fang sticking out of the monster's mouth.

4 Draw two large circles for eyes. Add two smaller circles for pupils. Draw detail lines on the horns.

Say "Yes" to Yetis!

This yeti is waving, "Hello!" from the mountain tops. Draw this friendly monster—and then draw him a friend!

1 Draw an egg shape for the monster's body. Add a square with rounded corners for the face. Then draw curved detail lines for the legs.

2 Add scalloped lines for the monster's hair and toes. Add curved lines for its arms.

3 Add more scalloped lines for the rest of the monster's hair. Add a half-circle to an arm for a hand.

4 Draw four ovals for fingers. Add two circles for eyes and a large half-oval for a mouth.

5 Draw a half-circle on the monster's hand. Add small circles to the eyes for pupils. Then add detail lines to the monster's mouth and toes.

Final

Fangy Friend

This little monster won't "bug" you at all! He has lots of little legs to get him wherever he needs to be. But what could those fangs be for?

Final

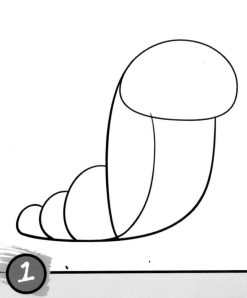

1

Draw a circle for the head. Add a pointed oval for the body. Sketch a curved detail line through the center of the body. Add three more curved lines for the rest of the bug's body.

2

Use detail lines to give the bug two antennas. Add a curved line for the bug's jaw. Draw curved lines along the bug's back. Then add a few thin ovals for spikes.

3

Add more thin ovals to bug's tail. Draw a curved line with a jagged line underneath to make a fang. Repeat to make a second fang. Sketch two circles for eyes. Add a scalloped line along the bug's stomach.

4

Add the last few back spikes. Draw very thin ovals for the bug's legs. Sketch long, slightly curved lines along the bug's stomach. Finish with small circles for pupils and a few detail dots for a nose.

Deep Sea Diver

Is this fanged fish friend or foe?
It's up to you and your pen to decide!

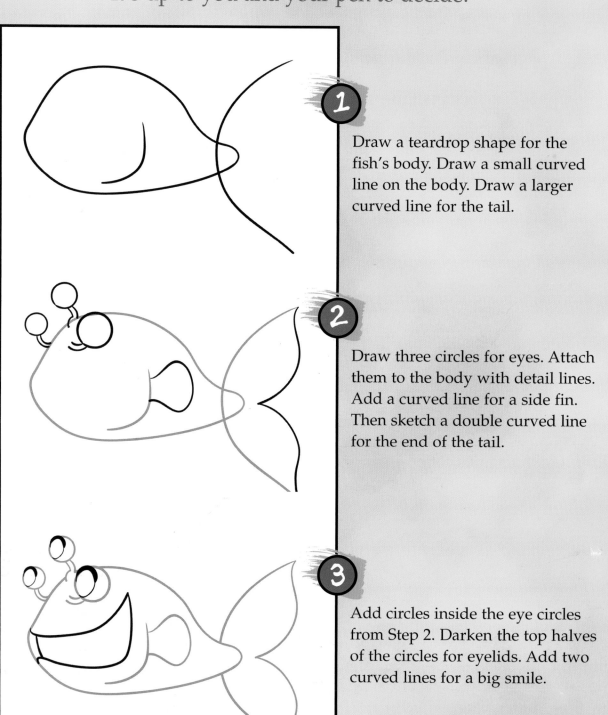

1 Draw a teardrop shape for the fish's body. Draw a small curved line on the body. Draw a larger curved line for the tail.

2 Draw three circles for eyes. Attach them to the body with detail lines. Add a curved line for a side fin. Then sketch a double curved line for the end of the tail.

3 Add circles inside the eye circles from Step 2. Darken the top halves of the circles for eyelids. Add two curved lines for a big smile.

4 Add spiked lines for the fish's back fins and teeth. Add detail lines for the fish's grin and bottom fin.

5 Add detail lines to all the fish's fins. Draw circles inside the eyes for pupils.

Final

Read More

Masiello, Ralph. *Ralph Masiello's Alien Drawing Book.* Watertown, Mass.: Charlesbridge, 2014.

Silvani, James. *Draw-a-Saurus: Everything You Need to Know to Draw Your Favorite Dinosaurs.* Berkeley, Calif.: Watson-Guptill, 2014.

Internet Sites

FactHound offers a safe, fun way to find Internet sites related to this book. All of the sites on FactHound have been researched by our staff.

Here's all you do:

Visit *www.facthound.com*

Type in this code: 9781491402825

Super-cool stuff!

Check out projects, games and lots more at www.capstonekids.com